*Voices From The Past* ✶ ✶ ✶ ✶ ✶ ✶ ✶ ✶ ✶ ✶

# KOREAN WAR

## KATHLYN GAY    MARTIN GAY

*Twenty-First Century Books*
*A Division of Henry Holt and Company*
*New York*

Twenty-First Century Books
A Division of Henry Holt and Company, Inc.
115 West 18th Street
New York, NY 10011

Henry Holt® and colophon are trademarks of
Henry Holt and Company, Inc.
*Publishers since 1866*

**Library of Congress Cataloging-in-Publication Data**
Gay , Kathlyn.
Korean War / Kathlyn Gay and Martin Gay.—1st ed.
p.    cm.—(Voices from the past)
Includes bibliographical references and index.
1. Korean War, 1950–1953—Juvenile literature. I. Gay, Martin, 1950–
II. Title. III. Series: Gay, Kathlyn. Voices from the past.
DS918.G36    1996
951.904'2—dc20                                              96-15577
                                                                CIP
                                                                AC

ISBN 0-8050-4100-1
First Edition—1996

Printed in the United States of America
All first editions are printed on acid-free paper. ∞
1 3 5 7 9 10 8 6 4 2

*Cover design by Karen Quigley*
*Interior design by Kelly Soong*

Cover: *Cowboy Artillery at Sooyang* by Mort Künstler
Courtesy of National Guard Heritage Series, Dept. of the Army,
National Guard Bureau, Washington, D.C.

**Photo credits**
pp. 7, 18: AP/Wide World Photos; pp. 15, 53: U.S. Naval Institute Collection;
pp. 21, 34-35, 42: UPI/Corbis-Bettmann; p. 27: U.S. Army Signal Corps/MacArthur
Memorial; pp. 31, 38: U.S. Army/AP-Wide World Photos; pp. 47, 56: Photri, Inc.;
p. 51: Corbis-Bettmann.

# Contents

| | | |
|---|---|---|
| *One* | A DIVIDED COUNTRY | 5 |
| *Two* | THE FALL OF SEOUL | 12 |
| *Three* | THE UN RESPONSE | 19 |
| *Four* | THE PUSAN DEFENSE | 25 |
| *Five* | COUNTERSTRIKE | 33 |
| *Six* | NORTH AND BACK AGAIN | 40 |
| *Seven* | THE END? | 46 |
| *Source Notes* | | 58 |
| *For Further Information* | | 61 |
| *Index* | | 63 |

| Date | Action | Date | Action |
|------|--------|------|--------|
| June 25, 1950 . . | North Korea invades South Korea; ignores UN demand that the Communists stop fighting and retreat to 38th parallel. | Jan. 16, 1951 . . . | Allies move north and reoccupy Seoul on Mar. 14. |
| June 27, 1950 . . | President Truman orders U.S. air and naval forces to South Korea. UN asks its members to aid South Korea. | Apr. 11, 1951 . . | Truman removes MacArthur from command. |
| | | July 10, 1951 . . . | Truce talks begin, but fighting continues. |
| June 30, 1950 . . | Truman orders ground forces into action. | Apr. 28, 1952 . . | Communist negotiators refuse to allow voluntary repatriation of prisoners. |
| July 5, 1950 . . . | American troops first meet North Koreans at Osan. | Oct. 8, 1952 . . . | Truce talks are broken off. |
| Sept. 8, 1950 . . | Allied troops stop the Communist advance at the Pusan Perimeter. | Mar. 28, 1953 . . | UN proposes an exchange of sick and wounded prisoners; Communists accept. |
| Sept. 15, 1950 . . | Allied troops land at Inchon. | | |
| Sept. 26, 1950 . . | UN forces under General MacArthur capture Seoul. | Apr. 26, 1953 . . | Truce talks resume. |
| Oct. 19, 1950 . . | Allies capture Pyongyang, North Korean capital. | July 27, 1953 . . . | Armistice agreement signed. Fighting stops. |
| Oct. 25, 1950 . . | China enters war. U.S. and Chinese troops meet at Changjin Reservoir and at Onjong. The Chinese withdraw on Nov. 6. | 1954 . . . . . . . . | Attempts to establish a permanent peace plan fail. |
| Nov. 26-7, 1950 | Chinese attack Allies and force an extended retreat. | | |

CHINA

RUSSIA

Chongjin

Yalu River

Changjin Reservoir

Chosan

NORTH KOREA

Yalu River

Sinuiju

Hamhung

Hungnam

Korea Bay

★ Pyongyang

▲

Wonsan

Sea of Japan

Taebaek Mtns.

▲ Nampo

Heartbreak Ridge

← Armistice Line

Panmunjom

▲ Punchbowl

Kaesong

38th Parallel

★ Seoul

Chuncheon

Inchon

▲

Wolmi-do

River Han

• Wonju

▲ Osan

Taebaek Mtns.

SOUTH KOREA

Chongju

Taebaek

Yellow Sea

Taejon

• Yechon

Naktong River

▲ Battles

Chonju

• Taegu

0        100 Miles

0        100 Kilometers

• Chonju

Chinju

Masan

Kwangju

Pusan

Mokpo

JAPAN

## One

✦

## $\mathcal{A}$ DIVIDED COUNTRY

$\mathcal{K}$im Chonggi was just eight years old when he and his older brother, Yonggi, and their parents moved into a house on the slope of a hill in Seoul, the capital city of the Republic of Korea. Chonggi's father (known by the family name Kim, which in Korea comes before a given name) had worked many years for a hat seller. He had been able to provide a comfortable life for his family, putting aside enough money to purchase the house and settle into it just as World War II was coming to a close in 1945. The Allies (which included the United States, Great Britain, and Russia—the Union of Soviet Socialist Republics, known as the USSR) had fought the Axis powers made up of Germany, Japan, Italy, and several other nations.

Like many people worldwide, the Kim family eagerly awaited the end of the war, which they hoped would also end Japanese domination. For decades, the Koreans had been under the harsh rule of the Japanese, who had taken control of the country in 1910, making it part of Japan. During the long period of brutal colonization, the Japanese tried to destroy Korean culture; they discriminated against Koreans in jobs, education, and politics. Even the Korean language and names were outlawed.

The Allies had promised repeatedly that Korea would

become free and independent when the Japanese were finally defeated. But the Soviets had other plans for Korea, with which it shared a border. The communist regime of the Soviet Union, headed by Joseph Stalin, wanted a foothold in Korea after the war, so just days before the Japanese surrender, the Soviet Union declared war on Japan. Twice before the two nations had gone to war over Korea and neighboring territories, but Japan had come away with the spoils each time.

## THE DIVIDING LINE

After Japan surrendered in August 1945, some Japanese troops continued to maintain control in Korea, and U.S. officials met with the Soviets to decide how the Japanese would be disarmed. Because Stalin had publicly supported the sovereign right of Koreans to establish their own government with free elections, Americans agreed to Soviet occupation of the north while the United States occupied the southern part of the Korean Peninsula.

To determine the boundary between north and south, officials looked at a map and chose the 38th parallel of north latitude as the dividing line. This cut the peninsula almost in half.

Donald Chung, who was a medical student at the time, reported what transpired when the Red Army, named for the Soviet's red flag, marched into North Korea. The army

> was accompanied by a cadre of Korean Communists. Under the guns of the Soviet troops, a Communist-controlled provisional government was quickly established by the simple means of placing Korean Communists in key positions of authority. The sealing of the 38th Parallel began almost immediately.[1]

In short, the two sections of Korea were virtually two different nations. Numerous efforts were made to reunify Korea, but they all failed. Nevertheless, in 1947 the United States asked the United Nations (UN) to supervise countrywide free elections, hoping Koreans would be able to establish their own national government. The UN had been chartered two years earlier as a way for nations to work together for world peace. However, Soviet guards along the border between the two sections of Korea would not allow UN observers to cross north of the 38th parallel. In fact, guards prevented anyone from going either way across the demarcation line.

On August 15, 1948, elections were finally held in the southern part of the country, and American-backed Syngman Rhee, who was educated in the United States, was named president of the Republic of Korea, as it was officially known. U.S. occupying forces pulled out, but the United

*General Douglas MacArthur* (left), *supreme Allied commander in Japan, and  Syngman Rhee* (right), *president of the Republic of Korea*

States left about 500 military advisers to support the new army known as the ROKs.

Meanwhile in the north, communists formed the Democratic People's Republic of Korea (DPRK), proclaiming it to be the legitimate government of all Koreans, with its capital in Pyongyang, North Korea. Although an election was held in September 1948, only members of the Communist Party were allowed to vote, and Kim Il Sung became premier. The new premier's real name was Kim Sung Chu, but he called himself Kim Il Sung after a legendary warrior who had died fighting the Japanese invaders years before. In late 1948, the Soviet Union moved most of its troops out of the territory but made certain that the North Korean Army was very well trained and equipped with the latest guns, artillery, and heavy tanks—quite the opposite of the situation in South Korea.

## REMAKING A PEOPLE

Besides the military hardware and political and financial support, the Soviet Union also provided the ideological basis for the organization of the Democratic People's Republic in the north. Kim Il Sung, power hungry and opportunistic, used the rhetoric and command structure of the Soviet communists to remake North Korean society.

The government's edicts affected everyone, including students like Donald Chung at the medical school. Even though they were being trained to become doctors, the students were still required to attend military classes, which "were held every day, rain or shine." As Chung wrote, "If it rained, we simply did our crawling and marching through the mud. We were sometimes called out for night sessions of simulated combat, usually with mud daubed on our faces to make us invisible in the moonlight." Students were also required to study communist principles developed by Karl Marx, a philosopher, and Vladimir I. Ulyanov, who called himself Lenin, the first communist dictator in Russia. In Chung's words:

> The "correct" ideological orientation of students had a high priority. Our main text for this course was a history of the Russian Communist Party . . . and we were expected to know all the details by memory. . . . We were further taught to hate imperialism, mainly the brand promulgated by the United States and the Syngman Rhee government of South Korea.[2]

By 1950, most people living under the flag of the DPRK viewed the ROK government as nothing more than a puppet of the "United States Imperialists." Many were convinced that the United States would back the south in an invasion of the north, and they were more than willing to support Kim Il Sung in his quest to "defend the Korean People's Democratic Republic and its constitution; [and]. . . liquidate the unpatriotic fascist puppet regime of Syngman Rhee which has been established in the southern part of the republic."[3]

Those living in the south were also being warned of an invasion. They were told horror stories about communist aggressors and what they would do to innocent people if they ever did invade the south to reunify the country. With so much propaganda being broadcast from one side of the 38th parallel to the other, there was general concern that armed conflict between the north and south might erupt soon. Indeed, both sides threatened war, and numerous skirmishes took place on the border between the two sections.

Chonggi's big brother was one of those who was certain war was near. As Yonggi wrote:

I don't want a war, but war is approaching. They have been talking about it for sometime now. An Army officer has boasted that we can seize Pyongyang in a matter of days. It may or may not be true, I am almost sure that we shall win in the long run. At any rate, it would be wiser for either side not to start one. For our part, we have been building up our military strength with American aid, but who knows what they have been doing in the north? They are far shrewder than us, the Communists.[4]

## THE SURPRISE INVASION

In June 1950, North Korean forces were estimated at between 150,000 and 200,000 troops, including ten infantry divisions, one tank division, and an air force division. In contrast, the ROKs (the South Korean forces) were a poorly equipped force of less than 100,000 men with very few tanks, heavy artillery, or combat airplanes. On the night of June 24, just under 100,000 North Korean soldiers with tanks and heavy artillery were taking up positions a few hundred yards north of the 38th parallel. Many thousands more were being held at the ready reserve. Unaware of this activity, only 40,000 ROK soldiers were stationed along the entire southern portion of the boundary line.

The Kim family went to bed as usual that night, suspecting nothing. "The day of June the twenty-fifth broke quietly as if all was right in God's world," wrote Chonggi, adding:

Being Sunday, I remained in bed with Big Brother for an hour or two longer than ordinary. . . . Came noon. Big brother had gone out somewhere. I, too, set forth to see a friend of mine in Kalwol Dong. By the time I came upon the Huam market-place, I became aware of something unusual in the air. People were gathered in fives and sixes, speaking in loud, excited voices. Then I saw trucks overloaded with soldiers. The soldiers had camouflage twigs, boughs and grass on their caps, the trucks were running at full speed, trailing sirens and raising dust. . . . Approaching a middle-aged gentleman who stood apart beside a telegraph pole, apparently to hail a taxi, I asked him shyly what was going on. The man, who looked nervous and agitated, gave me the answer in one word: "War."

"What war would it be, sir?" I asked again.

"The Communists, my boy, have invaded us across the thirty-eighth parallel."[5]

*Two*

# THE FALL OF SEOUL

*M*ost residents of Seoul thought the action on the 38th parallel was just another one of the many intermittent border skirmishes. Both sides had intruded on each other's territory, making raids to test enemy strength and attempting to gain whatever small advantage they could in position. Some in Seoul wondered if the fighting might be an extension of the South Korean internal conflict. There had been numerous armed attempts to unseat the Rhee government, and those clashes had already claimed 30,000 lives. But it soon became obvious that the June 25 incursion was something very different indeed.

Some 90,000 troops of the North Korean People's Army (NKPA) poured over the border into South Korea at five strategic points. Many of these men were battle hardened from duty with the Communist Chinese or Soviets in Manchuria during World War II. They followed the lead of 150 Russian-built heavy T-34 tanks that were almost impervious to the small-arms fire that was the limit of the ROK army's meager defense. The action was such a surprise and so well conceived with superior numbers, experience, and equipment that the South Koreans were soon in full retreat. They rushed back to defend the capital, Seoul.

To this day scholars argue over the reasons why the

north invaded the south, starting a civil war in Korea. Most experts agree, however, that since the United States had withdrawn its direct military presence and had made statements implying that Korea was not of strategic importance, Kim Il Sung saw an opportunity to quickly reunify his nation by force. He nearly succeeded.

## IN FLIGHT

The people of the capital, including Chonggi's family, tensely waited for word about the troops bearing down on their city. For the Kims, the fear of attack was one more peril they had been forced to endure during the changes taking place in Korea. Chonggi's father had lost his job because his employer, a Japanese man who had come to Korea to make his fortune, was no longer welcome. Like many other Japanese, he was forced to leave Korea after Japan's defeat.

Writing later about the experiences he endured in the hectic first few months of 1950, Kim Chonggi noted, "Before long . . . Father's savings ran out out and out. He used to go to seek some employment only to be turned down at one place after another. . . . [He] eventually obtained a position in the Government [of the Republic of Korea] through the good offices of an old and influential friend."[1]

With the threat of invasion, however, the new job brought no relief to the Kim family. Chonggi's brother joined friends who were volunteering to take up arms with the ROK regulars. His father left the household and was missing for days but finally returned to announce that he had become an officer in the North Korean forces, a revelation that shocked Chonggi.

After Chonggi's father and brother took up arms to fight on opposite sides, the young boy was left to wait out the advance of the communists with his terrified mother. "We were so frightened," he remembered, "so terribly scared. There in a big house once filled with men and security, were just the two of us, a woman and a little boy, feeling like the only individuals marooned on a desert island."[2]

Chonggi and his mother had good reason to feel abandoned. As North Korean tanks and men approached the undefended city, thousands of people jammed the streets, trying to escape. Some trudged with bundles in hand or on their back, others led oxcarts, rode bicycles, or drove trucks toward the River Han and a bridge that led to safety on the south bank.

Some U.S. troops and officers as well as four American journalists had been ordered to evacuate their headquarters and get out of the city along the same route. One of the journalists in the crowd was Marguerite "Maggie" Higgins of the New York *Herald Tribune*, the only woman among 131 war correspondents covering the war in Korea. Although most of the military believed women belonged behind the lines and many had tried to prevent Maggie from going to battlefronts, this thirty-year-old woman, who had covered battles in the latter part of World War II, was able to maintain her place as an accredited reporter on the scene. On the night of evacuation, Higgins and a UN official jumped into a jeep to follow the other U.S. correspondents traveling in another jeep toward the river.

Keyes Beech of the *Chicago Daily News* and his companions from the *New York Times* and *Time* magazine got to the middle of a bridge where they were stalled amongst a mass of refugees. Then, as Keyes reported, there was a huge explosion and "a burst of orange flame; silhouetted against the flame was a truckload of Korean soldiers. The truck lifted into the air. I felt our jeep in motion—backwards."[3]

The bridge buckled in the middle, plunging people and vehicles into the river. Hundreds were killed or injured.

*Marguerite Higgins, here interviewing*
*Brigadier General John S. Bradley in Korea in 1951,*
*had also worked as a correspondent in World War II.*

Although Beech's companions suffered cuts from the shattered glass of the jeep's windshield, all of the men made it to safety as did Higgins, whose driver quickly turned around before reaching the melee on the bridge. They headed toward another route out of the city. Early the next morning, with her typewriter on the hood of a jeep, she typed out her dispatch for the *Herald Tribune*.

Higgins and the other reporters learned that the explosion was the result of an ill-timed bombing. A ROK commander, desperately trying to slow the advance of North Koreans, had ordered his South Korean soldiers to blow up the bridge too soon. The action was planned to provide time for the Rhee government to reestablish headquarters farther south, but with the premature explosion, many supplies, trucks, and other matériel were lost, along with troops. And many South Korean troops were stranded on the north side of the river, forcing them to use ferries or rowboats to get to the south bank.

## OCCUPATION

North Korean occupying forces set up a government in Seoul, while the NKPA continued to grind south, virtually unopposed, toward the tip of the peninsula. Only 100,000 residents had been able to evacuate the city, and the remaining million and a half were under the control of the communists.

Kun-Ho Lee, a respected author on Korean law, was a resident of Seoul during that time, and he and his family, which included four children and an elderly grandparent, decided against escape and stayed in their home. He reported that after the communist army took over the city, "the walls were plastered with posters of 'Peoples's Army, Mansei!' and a stern order for the display of the Communist flag was issued. . . . Pictures of Kim Il Sung and Stalin were at all the important places.[4]

The occupation was very hard on anyone who had written or spoken out against the communists. Many liberals, educators, former government officials, and persons thought to pose a threat to the new communist order were arrested. When dissidents were captured, a mock trial like the one described in Kun-Ho Lee's account took place:

> The Communists with rifles and burp guns brought in a number of bound young men, and said, "Now we are going to begin the People's Court." Afterwards an accuser with an armband would relate the charges against a prisoner, specifying the punishment as death . . . he asked if anyone was opposed to it. Who would dare say anything in opposition even though all the people gathered there felt it was not right and pitied the victim. Opposition meant losing one's own life. The onlookers were as silent as a dead mouse. Then the fellow with the armband said, "I recognize that you all favor it. The execution will take place right here." So saying he made the victim sit down with his back turned and they shot him.[5]

As the occupation continued, refugees still managed to escape and move south toward the Republic of Korea boundary lines. Chonggi's mother finally decided to leave with her boy when their situation seemed impossible to endure. Food was almost nonexistent, and there was no money and no word from Chonggi's brother or father. Although she was very ill, Chonggi's mother took her son and joined the ranks of refugees making their way out of the city on foot. Chonggi recalled:

> Each time I saw a complete family, father, mother and children, I envied them. . . . We reached Pyongtaek three days

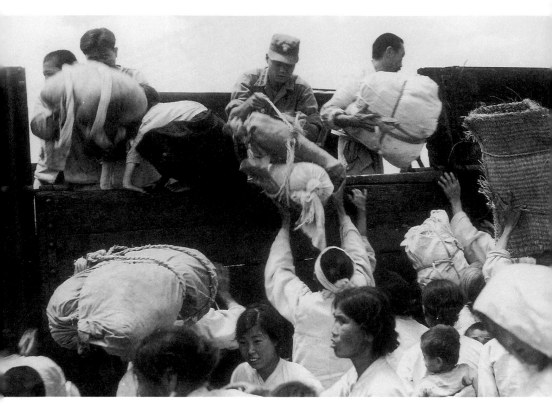

*Korean civilians are aided by a Republic of Korea soldier*
*as they board a train to flee from Communist troops.*

later, barely making it. . . . We had not a bite of food, nor a drink of warm water that whole day. Mother was steadily weakening. I did not know what to do. I continually asked her if she was all right, and she repeatedly said she was dying and that she was sorry to have to leave me behind all by myself. I begged her to live: and, in the thickening night, I prayed for speedy break of day.

Mother died in my arms that night.[6]

## Three

# THE UN RESPONSE

By the evening of June 25, U.S. President Harry S. Truman had met with his most trusted advisers. The United States had to decide quickly what the North Korean attack meant—up to that time the policy in the White House had been to concentrate on the Soviet Union's plans for expansion in Europe. Since the end of World War II, the United States, Britain, and other European allies had become increasingly suspicious of and hostile toward the Soviet Union, waging a cold war—hostilities that stopped just short of open-armed conflict.

When the Soviet-backed North Korean communists overran the border into the Republic of Korea, many thought the invasion was just a distraction to involve American forces far from the actual target of aggression. But some officials wondered if the invasion was more than that. What if the North Koreans, Communist Chinese, and Soviets were really beginning their plan for world domination here on the rocky peninsula of Korea? Was this actually the start of World War III?

At the very least, the advisers reasoned, U.S. forces must respond quickly in order to delay the possible fall of Asia to communism. The United Nations Security Council, called together by an emergency request of the United States, agreed. On June 27, 1950, the council issued a resolution condemning the actions of the Democratic People's Republic of Korea and called for "an immediate cessation of hostilities." Noting that the Republic of Korea had asked for UN help, the council recommended that the UN "furnish such assistance as may be necessary to repel the armed attack and to restore international peace and security in the area."[1]

## U.S. ACTION

Backed by the UN resolution, the Truman administration acted quickly to protect the South Koreans. Almost immediately after the incursion, seventy-year-old General Douglas MacArthur, supreme commander of Allied powers in Japan, commander in chief of U.S. Forces, Far East, and commanding general, U.S. Army, Far East, was given permission to set up air and naval support operations around Korea. He first sent the U.S. Seventh Fleet into the strait between Red (Communist) China and the Nationalist Chinese stronghold of Formosa Island, now called Taiwan. The United States wanted to be sure the friendly government of Formosa was not taken over by the superior forces of the communists on the mainland.

MacArthur then ordered the bombing of North Korean troops, although he was not officially authorized to do so until days later. MacArthur's action caused friction with the Truman administration, and it was the first of many differences between MacArthur and Truman about how to conduct what the president called a "police action." The general was convinced that fighting a limited war was impossible, but the U.S. government was very concerned about the real possibility of having to drop an atomic bomb on the Soviets if their air power was brought in to support the North Koreans.

*A delegation of women went to Washington, D.C.,*
*in August 1950 to protest the Korean War and*
*to urge President Truman to outlaw the atomic bomb.*

After MacArthur visited the outskirts of the onetime capital of South Korea in late June, he was even more certain in his view that all of Korea and continental Asia would fall to the communists. He sent a telegram to Truman that read in part, "The only assurance for holding the present line and the ability to regain later the lost ground is through the introduction of US ground combat forces."[2] The Truman administration decided to take action immediately, and troops and arms were soon on their way to stem the North Korean advance.

Besides the United States and the Republic of Korea, which fielded the largest forces in the south, fifteen other nations eventually responded to the call from the United Nations and placed their men and equipment under the command of General MacArthur and the Eighth United States Army in Korea. Australia, the United Kingdom, the Netherlands, New Zealand, Canada, France, the Philippines, Sweden, Turkey, Thailand, South Africa, India, Greece, Belgium, Luxembourg, Denmark, Colombia, Ethiopia, Norway, and Italy became part of the world's first multinational army fighting under the blue and white flag of the United Nations. However, the United States sent more than 90 percent of the troops, military equipment, and supplies.

## TASK FORCE SMITH

The First Battalion of the Twenty-fourth Infantry Division under Colonel Charles Smith was the first to get marching orders. Major General William Dean, commander of the Twenty-fourth Infantry, asked Smith to take his troops, totaling just over 400 men, from Japan to Korea to fight a delaying action. "When you get to Pusan, head for Taejon. We want to stop the North Koreans as far from Pusan as we can. Block the main road as far north as possible," Dean ordered.[3]

Pusan is on the southeastern coast of the Korean Peninsula. Strategically, for both opposing armies, it was Korea's best port and most important city. The North Koreans knew that if they could control the port and airfields around Pusan, the UN forces would have to fight their way onto the peninsula. MacArthur also saw how critical it was to hold Pusan, and he began efforts to set up a defensive perimeter as wide as possible around the city. In order to accomplish that, he needed more time for men and equipment to arrive. So the delay tactic assigned to "Task Force Smith" was crucial. Two crack North Korean divisions were already south of Seoul, looking for the main road to Pusan.

On July 4, General Dean met Smith and his battalion in Taejon, the temporary capital of South Korea. Dean had thought that Taejon would be a good place to make a stand and set up military headquarters to direct the defensive operations. He sent Smith's men, now increased to 540 soldiers, including artillerymen with five 105-millimeter howitzer cannons, to the hills of Osan, a city on the road to Seoul north of Taejon. It was here on July 5 that the first battle of the war involving American men would be fought, and it soon became obvious that Smith's small force could not hold back the NKPA soldiers led by the Russian tanks.

Robert Roy, an eighteen-year-old private in a heavy weapons company assigned to aid Smith's men, was on a high hill with a huge gun—"basically a big bazooka mounted on a tripod," as Roy described it. Early in the morning, he and four other men with him spotted tanks coming. Roy recalled years later that they had tried to stop the tanks with their gun, but their efforts were futile. Then one of the tanks fired and hit just in front of Roy and the other men. "All five of us were thrown back over the hill from the concussion and the earth hitting us in the face," Roy recalled. "Our ears were ringing. We were all disoriented, couldn't function at all for five or ten minutes."

As the tanks kept coming, Roy and the other gunners heard Smith's order to withdraw and they "took off down the hill. . . . Everybody just kept going, as fast as they could. Slipping and sliding through the rice paddies."[4] Roy eventually caught up with an infantry company heading south, but many of his artillery unit were captured by North Koreans and spent the rest of the war as prisoners. At least 150

Americans were killed in the delaying action that did not work.

The North Koreans quickly reported their perspective on the rout, pointing out that the American force "was obliged to leave all its equipment on the field and retreat. The defeat of 'invincible' United States Army troops gave the People's Army a proud sense of accomplishment."[5]

The loss at Osan was a blow to General Dean's plans to slow the enemy. He had hoped that a delay there would provide more time to bring in men to defend Taejon, which was located nearly halfway between Seoul and Pusan. But as the North Koreans bore down on Taejon, Dean realized that this was the point where they had to be held.

The NKPA Third and Fourth Divisions hit Taejon in wave after wave, using a tactic known as "refugee attacks." Many thousands of refugees from Seoul were still clogging the roads. The North Koreans forced large groups of these unarmed civilians into a tight pack, then used them as cover as they drove them into armed U.S. positions.

This tactic and the NKPA's superior numbers soon forced General Dean and his troops out of Taejon, ending fifteen days of hell for the division, which went into reserve positions farther south. But Dean was not so lucky. He fell down an embankment in the dark while searching for water for some of his wounded men. Knocked unconscious for hours, he finally awoke to discover that his arm was broken and his men were gone. He wandered for thirty-six days, many of them without food or water, looking for friendly forces. Eventually he was captured by the enemy and spent the remainder of the war in a prison camp. He did not know until the war was over that the Twenty-fourth Division had done its job. His men had delayed the advance long enough to get troops and firepower in position to establish the Pusan Perimeter.

*Four*

✦

# The Pusan Defensive

$L$ieutenant General Walton H. Walker, better known as Bulldog, commanded the Eighth Army in South Korea, and under his leadership the enemy advance was slowed on the two fronts formed by the Naktong River. The water made a natural barrier on the north and the west sides of the land controlled by the Eighth Army and the ROK forces: a southeastern section of approximately 500 square miles that contained the important port of Pusan and the city of Taegu, where the Rhee government and Walker's headquarters were located.

Establishing a perimeter just inside the entire length of the Naktong, Walker planned to defend this last remaining bit of South Korea from any further North Korean advance. He was aided greatly by ground troops who arrived by the thousands from the United States and by the air power of U.S. Far East Air Forces. The Fifth Air Force, commanded by Major General Earl Partridge, worked hand in hand with Walker's ground troops to stop enemy forces wherever they threatened to break through the defensive line strung very thinly along the Naktong.

From the second day of fighting, the Fifth Air Force flew missions over Korea. At first they sent big transports to Seoul to evacuate American civilians who were about to be trapped. For support, fast-moving fighters accompanied the lumbering unarmed transport planes. On June 27, Americans registered their first "kill" of a Russian-built fighter that had tried to shoot down the retreating planes.

The air force missions were more than defensive in nature, however. Americans also made bombing runs north of the 38th parallel. Donald Chung described what happened in the town where he was going to medical school:

> News soon arrived that United States Air Force B-29 bombers had strewn hundreds of 500-pound bombs all across Chongjin, which was one of North Korea's major ports, a major steel-manufacturing center and the site of a Soviet-supported military supply complex. While the North Korean military authorities had been basking in the glory of their daily victories in the South, no serious thought had been given to the fact that the entire Korean peninsula could be reached by United States Air Force squadrons based in Japan.

The student body was ordered into trucks and then transported to downtown Chongjin, which was devastated by the U.S. bombs. Smoke still hung thickly in the air as Donald arrived:

> Hundreds of civilians—old, young, men, women, babies—lay dead or badly wounded in the twisted rubble. Many had bloody heads and faces while others had crushed or twisted limbs. . . . Everywhere, arms, legs, heads and other parts of human bodies protruded from heaps of rubble and fallen concrete and balls of crazed steel reinforcing rods.[1]

## "REMEMBER YECHON"

The first successful counterattack of the Korean War was launched at Yechon, an important road hub about fifty miles northeast of Taegu. Yechon had been captured by the North Koreans, and General Walker ordered the U.S. Twenty-fifth Infantry Division to drive them out. On July 20, 1950, the division's Twenty-fourth Infantry Regiment, a segregated unit made up of several battalions of all black soldiers, seized the town and turned over captured troops to the ROK.

"This was the first major victory for the U.S. Army in the Korean War," wrote Lieutenant Colonel Charles M. Bussey in his book about the war and the Yechon Battle. He noted that the victory "was hailed in the press and in the U.S.

*Troops from the Twenty-fourth Infantry Regiment*
*rest near the Han River crossing.*

Congress."[2] And on the battlefield, the slogan "Remember Yechon" was frequently used thereafter to build morale among troops. But according to Bussey,

> most historians of the Korean War have either dismissed this combat engagement or termed it a disgraceful defeat for the black troops. The U.S. Army's official history implies that there was no victory or even a real battle at Yechon.
>
> Despite evidence to the contrary, including first-hand reports by Associated Press (AP) correspondent Tom Lambert, this error has been perpetrated over the years by historians too careless to search out primary historical sources. It was not until Clay Blair published his *The Forgotten War* in 1987 that the facts about Yechon came out.[3]

Other instances of ignoring accomplishments of U.S. black soldiers also have surfaced in the years since the Korean War. As in previous wars involving Americans, many blacks who fought in Korea and deserved medals were overlooked or their heroism was diminished because some white officials did not want blacks to rise above the demeaning status U.S. society had established for people of color.

## THE PERIMETER WAR

The U.S. Marines were credited with the first official victory of the war. In the first week of August 1950, the North Koreans' powerful Sixth Division made a concerted attack near the town of Masan, located about fifty miles west of Pusan. It was do or die for the Eighth Army now.

General Walker's greatest concern within the Pusan Perimeter was the protection of the fifty-mile length of road that ran south from Taegu to Pusan. If the North Korean forces could cut this vital link, the city of Taegu and the entire region would likely fall. That would spell certain defeat for Walker's army. By using his ground troops and the air strikes on a priority basis, taking on the biggest battles first, he was able to keep the incessant North Korean attackers at bay all along the perimeter.

Walker sent a task force, made up of the Twenty-fifth Division led by Major General William Kean, to drive North Korean soldiers back. The counterattack was spearheaded by the newly arrived First Provisional Marine Brigade and their supporting air units. This cocky brigade of 6,000 men was well trained and full of veterans who had seen action in World War II. They were not about to lose the war here. As their commander, Brigadier General Edward Craig, put it when he addressed the men before they went out to engage the enemy, "The Pusan perimeter is like a weakened dike. It will be costly fighting against an enemy that outnumbers us. Marines have never lost a battle. This Brigade will not be the first one to do so."[4]

Craig was right. Using Pershing tanks that were a good match for the North Korean T-34s, the marines pressed forward to stop the enemy advance. Marine Corsairs (single-seat fighter planes) taking off from aircraft carriers in the Sea of Japan attacked the NKPA positions with bombs and machine gun fire. The marines led a rout of the North Koreans, pushing them twenty-six miles to the rear.

## NO-NAME RIDGE

After the Masan campaign, the marines had no time to celebrate their success. The North Koreans were now concentrated farther north and were threatening to overrun Miryang midway between Taegu and Pusan in an area known as the Naktong River Bulge. The marine brigade was sent to plug the hole in the line. A British officer, who saw the leathernecks (named for the leather band that was once part of their uniform) move out on August 16, described his feelings about the critical situation in a letter to his superiors:

> If Miryang is lost Taegu becomes untenable and we will be faced with a withdrawal from Korea. I am heartened that the Marine Brigade will move against the salient [battle line] tomorrow. They are faced with impossible odds, and I have no valid reason to substantiate it, but I have a feeling they will halt the enemy.[5]

The area of the "bulge" where the marines were heading was a ridge shown on the maps as Obong-ni. Place-names were tongue twisters for most Americans and places indicated on old charts were often inaccurate. So an American marine sergeant looked at Obong-ni written on his map and reportedly shouted in frustration, "The devil with that! It's No-Name Ridge. Now let's take it!"[6] And take it they did, but not without a fierce fight and terrible losses.

On the first day, the marines made two assaults up the hills that made up No-Name Ridge, but twice they were forced to retreat because of heavy fire. By nightfall, however, the tenacious marines had reached their objective. The next day, after air support from the Corsairs, which knocked out a strategically placed machine gun nest, they pushed the North Koreans off the ridge and finally back across the Naktong River.

More than 4,000 NKPA troops were found dead after the terrible battle, but the North Koreans were still not finished. Time and time again they launched new attacks against the Pusan Perimeter. Using a "human wave" tactic, thousands of well-armed North Koreans would charge a position and most would be cut down in withering Eighth Army firepower or by air-support strikes from the air force.

*North Koreans used Russian-made arms in many cases. This Russian machine gun was captured by U.S. forces during battle.*

But once that wave was ended, a second wave of thousands more troops, this time unarmed, would take their place. The NKPA had experienced losses in excess of 58,000 in the first months of the war, and many soldiers no longer had weapons. The second wave would have to pick up guns and ammunition from their fallen comrades in order to press the fight. But these suicide attacks were ineffective.

In September 1950 the UN forces numbered 180,000 under General Walker's command. Some 1,500 British soldiers had arrived, and the ROK had been reestablished with 91,500 South Koreans in service. With the air superiority supplied by the Marine Corsairs and the American, British, and Australian Air Forces, the North Korean threat was finally being handled at the perimeter.

The NKPA, however, kept pounding away at the line as they tried to get to Pusan. They were about to be surprised by a daring countermeasure.

## Five

# COUNTERSTRIKE

*G*eneral quarters already had been sounded throughout the carrier," wrote Lieutenant Commander Max Miller, recalling events on the *Sicily*, a U.S. ship transporting jeeps to Korea. General quarters, an alarm signaling sailors to go to their battle stations and stand ready for action, was not unusual. As Miller reported, it "sounded every morning at sea an hour before sunrise."[1] But this was to be a very important day—the beginning of Operation Chromite, the surprise amphibious attack on Inchon Harbor.

On the *Sicily*, men were readying the Marine Corsairs in the port and starboard catapults for launches that would start the attack on Wolmi-do, a small fortified island that guarded the entrance to Inchon's treacherous harbor. Miller reported:

> The fliers had been prepared well ahead of time, of course, for the scheduled moment of the first take-off strike . . . the props were spinning with the warm-up. . . . The first pilot, after revving his motor and testing all odds and ends, indicated that he was ready to be shot off . . . with [a] fast gesture mindful of a quick salute, and with equal quickness he then jammed his head back against the head-rest in preparation for the catapult shock. With the whang of the cable he

was away and off, his plane loaded with all the rockets and napalms [incendiary material dropped from planes] it could carry. . . . This first strike . . . had been assigned the task of burning off the island of Wolmi-Do, preparatory for the Marine landings.[2]

Taking Wolmi-do was the critical first step in a bold counter-attack that had been first formulated by General MacArthur in the early days after the NKPA invasion. The general had no support from either his superiors in the U.S. Joint Chiefs of Staff or his own inner circle for the deployment of more than 28,000 men by sea into Inchon, one of the most difficult embarking points on the coast.

*A U.S. Navy Corsair on combat air patrol over UN warships in Inchon harbor*

Harry Summers Jr. was in the U.S. Infantry during the war, and he explained the problem of Inchon in his *Korean War Almanac*:

> The port of Inchon, which serves the capital city of Seoul, is located not quite half-way up Korea's western coast on the Yellow Sea. The entire Yellow Sea is shallow, and tidal differences range from 20 to 40 feet. At Inchon the tide ranges from 23 feet to 35 feet; at low tide the entire inner harbor is reduced to a vast swamp of mud flats.[3]

Although there was danger that the landing craft could be stranded, MacArthur was certain the attack would catch the

North Koreans by surprise. He argued for hours about the importance of his strategy. The invaders' supply lines were stretched dangerously thin from the 38th parallel through Seoul and down to the battlefront at the Pusan Perimeter, so MacArthur reasoned that a successful landing and the recapture of Seoul would cut the North Koreans' lifeline and turn the tide of war.

## THE TURN AROUND

The naval guns started blasting the island before sunrise, and the Corsairs and other air force planes made bombing runs and napalm drops on Wolmi-do and the surrounding area. By 0633 (6:33 A.M.) the marines had landed on the island, and at 0750 it was reported secured. The tide was receding, however, and the landing and support craft had to move away from the shore quickly, leaving the marines stranded until the second phase of the attack could commence on the next high tide, scheduled for later that evening.

Max Miller aboard the *Sicily* reported that "mudbanks reached out a mile or more from the shore proper. And the landing crafts which had gone in, including some of the large LSTs [landing ships carrying tanks], just had to stay wherever the low tide had caught them."[4]

Protected from the air and by the big sixteen-inch guns of vessels that had made it to deep water, the men and equipment survived the tense hours of September 15. In the late afternoon, the marines began the assault of Inchon proper. One attack was on Red Beach, and correspondent Marguerite Higgins was with a marine unit driving toward the area when she saw the effects of the assault on Wolmi-do. It was ablaze like "a forest fire had just swept over it," she reported. She could also see Red Beach just beyond and witnessed a rocket hitting an oil tank. "Big ugly smoke rings billowed up," she wrote. "The dockside buildings were brilliant with flames . . . it looked as if the whole city was burning."[5]

By 0130 on September 16, all of the objectives set for that first day were met. Inchon was captured, and only twenty Americans had perished in the attempt. It was a great victory and one of Douglas MacArthur's finest moments.

The victory also began to change the fortunes of everyone fighting in the southern portion of the Korean Peninsula. On September 28, the forces that had landed at Inchon, now numbering 50,000 men and 250,000 tons of equipment, cleared the final occupying troops out of the South Korean capital in a street-to-street battle that left much of the city in ruins. Meantime, Bulldog Walker had coordinated his men and equipment with the assault at Inchon, and the Eighth Army was prepared to break through the Pusan Perimeter and chase down the retreating North Korean troops who were trying to get back to the 38th parallel.

Many of the American, British, and South Korean troops were anxious to move north quickly and join in the rout of the North Korean forces. General Paik Sun Yup, commander of the Republic of Korea Army's First Division, which had seen valorous duty in defense of Pusan, knew his men wanted to get into the thick of the action. After the success of Inchon, he waited for orders to pursue the NKPA, but for several days they were assigned to mop-up operations—making sure the area was secure. He reported:

> We were in our third day of the mop-up when I ran into a U.S. unit [Task Force 777] at a crossroads on September 22, 1950. . . . It was commanded by Maj. Gen. Hobart Gay, commanding general of the U.S. 1st Cavalry Division. . . . "We're pushing north to the Osan area," General Gay told me, "to link up with U.S. X Corps that landed at Inchon." As Task

*General Paik Sun Yup* (left) *commanded the ROK Army's First Division. He is pictured here with U.S. Major General Laurence Cragie.*

Force 777 revved up, General Gay yelled out, "See you in Seoul!" The American unit moved out at a furious pace.

All I could do was stare in frustration at the column of U.S. tanks and trucks as the dust it kicked up wafted skyward like a beckoning cloud marking the road to North Korea.[6]

The ROK First Division did finally move north and was just a few days behind the ROK Third, which actually crossed the 38th parallel into North Korea on September 30, 1950. The

Inchon success had been so complete that all the goals set at the outset of the conflict were now accomplished. The North Korean invasion was repelled, and the capital was returned to the control of Syngman Rhee. It could be said that this war was won by the United States and its allies fighting under the sanctions of the United Nations resolutions—if only it had ended with Inchon.

## Six

# NORTH AND BACK AGAIN

*B*ecause General MacArthur had the tactical advantage during the fall of 1950, he wanted his men to keep pushing through North Korea toward the Chinese region of Manchuria just across the border between China and Korea. Newly appointed U.S. Secretary of Defense George Marshall supported this plan, even though the UN had authorized only ROK troops to cross the 38th parallel. Given MacArthur's incredible popularity after Inchon, the U.S. Joint Chiefs of Staff went along with his decision to invade.

General Walker was technically in charge of the Eighth Army and all of the allied troops, ROKs, and marine divisions on the ground in Korea, so he expected to direct the pursuit of the retreating NKPA troops. But MacArthur, over the objections of many of his subordinates, decided to split off the First Marines and Seventh Army Divisions and put them into a new unit called the X Corps. These forces, which had just taken Inchon and Seoul under General Edward Almond, were transported around the peninsula to make another amphibious landing at the important city of Wonsan, North Korea, on the eastern coast.

However, South Korean regulars known as the Rambling ROKs had already captured the city. This was especially frustrating to the X Corps Marines who had expected to make a triumphant landing at the port, then lead the advance up the eastern side of the peninsula while the Eighth Army moved up the western edge on the other side of the Taebaek Mountains. The object was to drive through to the Yalu River and the Chinese border.

## KIM IL SUNG ON THE RUN

In the west, the Eighth Army was made up of elements of the First Cavalry, several U.S. divisions, a British Commonwealth brigade, a Turkish brigade, battalions from the Philippines and Thailand, and four divisions of ROK troops. They were making real progress against almost no resistance. The North Korean capital of Pyonyang soon fell after heavy bombing by the air force and a spearhead invasion by the ROK First Division under General Paik Sun Yip. The General was from Pyonyang, and he described his arrival at his hometown as "the most exquisite in my life." But, he reported, as his men got closer to the city, they

> suddenly came under intense machine-gun and mortar fire, much of which seemed to be directed right at my head. It was a close thing. . . . I jumped down quickly from my tank and flopped unceremoniously down in a ditch along the road. The tank returned the fire, making short work of the enemy pocket.
>
> As our lead vehicles pulled into the intersection, an ear-splitting explosion came from the direction of the [Taedong River] bridge, and chunks of flying iron filled the air. The enemy had welcomed us to Pyonyang by blowing the bridge.[1]

The destruction of the bridge barely slowed the assault on the city, however. Right behind the ROK came Major General

Hobart Gay and his First Cavalry Division and a great deal of American military bra s with the international press.

Everything seemed to be going the allies' way, and MacArthur wanted to push on. Because Kim Il Sung was in flight to the far reaches of the north of his territory, MacArthur changed his objectives. His goal became the complete reunification of Korea. But in the United States, President Truman was deeply concerned about warnings coming from Communist China. Earlier, the Chinese had threatened to intervene in the Korean War if UN forces crossed the 38th parallel. At a meeting between Truman and General MacArthur on Wake Island on October 15, Truman wanted reassurance from the general that the Chinese would not launch a full-scale attack. MacArthur declared that there

*President Harry Truman met with General Douglas MacArthur on Wake Island in October 1950 to assess the trouble in Korea.*

was little chance of this and that the war would be over by Thanksgiving.

## SURPRISE ATTACK

The Eighth Army advance seemed to go very easily. Some resistance was reported, but it was sporadic and rare. Thousands of NKPA soldiers lost their will to fight and gave up en masse as the ROK First and Sixth Divisions pressed toward the Yalu River. Victory appeared certain, and parades were even planned in Tokyo at the army headquarters. But on October 25, 1950, the lead troops of the Eighth Army suddenly met stiff resistance, surprising those in command. As General Paik recalled, "No one knew that the communist Chinese Army had crossed the Yalu River into the Korean peninsula [during October 1950] and now lay in ambush in every nook and cranny of the rugged Jongyuryong Mountain Range."[2]

Roughly 130,000 Chinese soldiers were waiting for the UN troops. When the lead units of the Eighth Army got close to the Chinese border, some within sight of the Yalu, the Chinese forces (known as the Chinese Peoples' Volunteers in Korea) launched their first full-scale attack. On November 1, two divisions of the Chinese Thirteenth Army struck the ROK First Division's Fifteenth Infantry and the U.S. Army's Eighth Cavalry regiment of the First Cavalry Division. Both units were almost totally destroyed. The Chinese launched a second offensive on November 25, using eighteen divisions of the Thirteenth Army and sending the Eighth Army into full retreat.

## THE EASTERN FRONT

On the other side of the Taebaek Mountains, the X Corps was moving away from the relative safety of the port of

Wonsan following the lead of the First Marine Division. Their main objective was to get to the mountainous passes surrounding a huge lake called the Chongjin (or Chosin) Reservoir and from there head over the crests toward Manchuria, the northeastern region of China.

General Oliver Smith had already heard about the November 1 attack on the Eighth Army in the west, and he was very leery of stringing his troops in a long chain down miles of narrow roadway. General MacArthur still held to his very optimistic view that the Chinese were not sending in a strong force. He believed that the troops who were fighting in Korea were volunteers and Koreans who lived in China. In MacArthur's view the cavalry regiment and the ROK Fifteenth had been defeated because they were not prepared and had scattered in the dark.

General Smith was not convinced. He deliberately slowed his advance north. Besides, it was turning very cold in the mountains of North Korea, and the troops did not have adequate clothing to protect them from bitter winds and temperatures well below 0°F.

The First Marine Brigade, however, was ordered west to Yudam-ni. MacArthur sent a message to his troops announcing a massive offensive to end the war soon, and the X Corps was to meet up with the Eighth Army somewhere in the central part of the country. Together they would drive any resistance back across the Yalu. When the Fifth and Seventh Regiments reached the village of Yudam, however, about 100,000 Chinese were poised to destroy the 24,000 marines who were in a long line that stretched all the way back to the coast. The Chinese planned to cut the main supply route at various points and set up roadblocks. Then, with overpowering numbers, the Chinese troops expected to surround the marines trapped between the roadblocks and destroy each unit in turn.

On November 27, the Battle of Frozen Chosin (named for the huge reservoir) began. The Chinese forces attacked the outnumbered marines and wounded and killed many men as they struggled to get back to the defensive perimeter that had been established at Hagaru. Many of the men were near collapse, and as correspondent Higgins reported, some were dazed and "like men who had accepted death and then found themselves alive after all."[3]

Keyes Beech was also there on December 4, 1950, when

half a dozen shivering marine officers, their eyes and noses watery with cold, huddled around the fat tent stove for warmth. . . . It was 15 degrees below zero. . . . We were listening to a tall rangy man . . . Raymond Murray, commanding officer of the 5th Marine Regiment, one of the Corps' most illustrious fighting units.

Murray's words had a strange, unreal quality. For what he was saying was that the Marines were in retreat. Nothing like this, he explained with some wonder in his voice, had ever happened to the Marines before."[4]

## Seven

## 𝒯HE END?

𝒯he retreat south was difficult on both sides of the Taebaek Mountains. There were now 180,000 Communist Chinese troops crushing down on the totally out-manned allied units in the west. Another 120,000 were pressing the X Corps in the east. The Chinese clearly had the momentum in the war.

Delaying where they could, the Eighth Army and the X Corps continued to fall back toward the 38th parallel. Many Korean refugees clogged the roads, so moving men and equipment was a slow process and casualties were high. The Chinese plan to send great masses of their men down through the center of the peninsula to divide allied armies and attack east and west was very effective.

### U.S. REACTION

In the United States, critics of the war began to question General MacArthur's performance. In addition, because of the press reports of the defeat of the marines and the Eighth Army, 55 percent of Americans were convinced that World War III had begun, according to a Gallup Poll in December 1950.

The general's support from the Truman administra-

*The X Corps faced a bitter winter in early 1951.*

tion, never very firm, began to wither away, and the administration discussed using the atom bomb against the Chinese. U.S. officials were concerned that the Chinese attack might prompt the Soviet Union to enter the war. When MacArthur requested permission to send U.S. planes into Manchuria where the Chinese had sanctuary from the air force bombers, the Truman administration refused to spread the war into China's territory. The general then held a press conference and belligerently charged that Washington had lost its will to win.

Finally, the President had had enough. He fired MacArthur on April 11, 1951.

When MacArthur returned to the United States, he was greeted with a ticker tape parade, and there were calls for Truman's impeachment in Congress. But many men who fought the war had a more sobering impression of the "old soldier." James A. Frowein was one. He was drafted and served in the Korean conflict from April 1, 1952 until May 1953, and recently noted: "I was still at home when MacArthur was given the boot. I had heard too many stories about his colossal vanity to be moved to pity. I firmly believe that our democracy can only survive if the military is subject to the will of the people (government)."[1]

## THE "YO-YO WAR"

Two days before Christmas in December 1950, General Walker was killed in a jeep accident near the frontline. Lieutenant General Matthew B. Ridgway took over command of the Eighth Army, and one of his first priorities was to instill a fighting spirit into the demoralized men under his command. The Eighth Army had just completed the longest retreat in United States military history, and Ridgway had to stop the bleeding. He had little time, however. On January 1,

1951, seven Chinese armies moved against the UN line protecting Seoul. Three days later Seoul once again fell to the Communist forces.

Ridgway retreated, and with help from the X Corps he established a line across the peninsula just south of the capital city. A new offensive, nicknamed the Meatgrinder by the frontline troops, was launched on January 24 against tremendous enemy opposition. UN forces began to move the Chinese—now tired, cold, and without basic supplies—back toward the 38th parallel once again. The Chinese advance was stopped, and by April 22, Seoul was back in UN hands.

General Ridgway moved to Tokyo to replace General MacArthur, and Lieutenant General James A. Van Fleet took command of the Eighth Army. At the end of April he led his troops back over the 38th parallel once more—until the Chinese began another offensive. This time 450,000 Chinese troops pushed the Eighth Army back to just a few miles north of Seoul where Van Fleet was able to halt the advance. On May 10, the Chinese launched a second offensive against the eastern side of the line. In a surprisingly bold move, Van Fleet attacked in the west.

UN soldiers on the frontlines called all of the advances and retreats during the spring and on into the summer of 1951 the "yo-yo war." But eventually the UN forces were able to regain control of the territory they had lost, and the communists suffered their heaviest casualties of the war. By the end of May, the UN troops had forced the enemy to retreat, although they continued attacks to hold positions.

Ted White, along with the all-black Twenty-fourth Infantry Regiment, took part in several of those efforts to hold off the enemy. In June 1951, he was with a squad of twenty men ahead of the frontline. They dug foxholes into a hill and put two men and a machine gun in each. Equipped with pistols, rifles, and grenades and covered by artillery from the rear, the squad was told to hold the hill. The Chinese advanced at night, with huge numbers of soldiers coming at the UN forces. White, firing a machine gun, and the others on the hill fought all night long, yet the Chinese kept coming at them. At daylight the fighting stopped, and as White recalled,

> we could see what we'd done to them. There were dead Chinese all over the ground. Hundreds and hundreds of them. And they were only the ones their people couldn't drag away in the dark.
>
> Everybody on that hill was recommended for a Bronze Star. I never got one, but I understand the recommendation went in.[2]

## PEACE TALKS

In spite of enemy losses, Van Fleet's orders were clear: Do not press the advantage. He maintained control of the region around the 38th parallel and bolstered the security of the southern section of the peninsula. The enemy also began building heavily fortified defensive structures. It was now obvious that neither side would be able to win a total victory on the battlefield. It was time to talk.

A fitful start to armistice talks began in the North Korean town of Kaesong in July 1951. The United States, North Korea, and China sent representatives, but little agreement could be reached. The talks at Kaesong broke off in August. Fighting had not ended during the talks, but it had been limited to artillery fire and sniping from foxholes.

With the breakdown of discussions, furious fighting broke out again in late August in an area called the Punch Bowl, located in the east, just north of the UN line. Some of the bloodiest fighting of the war took place on a hillside known as Heartbreak Ridge in this region. Finally, the marines and the army gained control of the area, but casualties were horrendous.

Fighting continued unabated, carried on as "trench warfare," but in late October peace talks resumed at Panmunjom. Over time, many issues were resolved. A demarcation line and a demilitarized zone, known as the DMZ, were established between the two sections of Korea, but peace negotiators could not agree on the repatriation of prisoners of war (POWs).

*As part of the peace talks at Panmunjom, Communist negotiators agreed to the establishment of a demilitarized zone.*

The POW question was an important one for the United States. Conditions in the camps were horrible. In one camp alone, some 1,700 prisoners died from starvation and disease.

Among the captives were some civilians, including British, French, and Russian men and women, Roman Catholic priests and nuns, and men and women from a Methodist mission. They were held in camps along the Yalu. Not long after their capture, the civilians were forced along with POWs on a death march of more than one hundred miles to Chunggang-jin, over mountains and rugged, snowy terrain in the bitter cold. The North Korean major commanding the march ordered POW leaders "not to allow anyone to drop out. If you do, I will punish you with the extreme penalty of military discipline. Even the dead must be carried."[3] Anyone who fell by the wayside was shot, which was the fate of one of the nuns. North Korean guards kicked her body over a ridge, letting it roll down into a gully.

Nell Dyer of Arkansas, who had been with the Methodist mission, took charge of the aged and the sick women and often pleaded with North Korean guards to allow the elderly to rest. She even tried to appeal to the Korean tradition of respect for age, but a guard told her that because they were now in the People's Army, they were "not free in these matters anymore."[4]

Many stories about North Korean atrocities circulated from the earliest days of the war. Patrols had come across bodies of their compatriots, hands tied behind their backs, bullets in their heads, in direct violation of the Geneva Convention treaty, an agreement signed by many nations that provided for humane treatment of captured soldiers in war.

POWs were also subjected to "brainwashing." They

would be questioned for long periods, often forced to stand at attention day after day or subjected to other forms of torture. The intention was to force them to sign confessions about war crimes they did not commit or to join the communist army. All of these "conversions" could then be used by the North Korean or Communist Chinese propaganda campaigns to discredit the actions of the UN force and especially the United States.

*Prisoners at this POW camp in Korea*
*flew a UN flag that they had made.*

The UN insisted that all POWs be given the choice of returning to their home countries or defecting to the other side. But the communists were adamant that their soldiers be returned, whether or not they wanted to be. About 60,000 of the 130,000 prisoners in South Korean camps had signed papers refusing repatriation, and during May 1952, communist POWs staged a series of riots to protest any forced return to life under the communists.

## A FORGOTTEN WAR?

About this time, changes occurred in the UN military command, with General Mark W. Clark replacing Ridgway. In an attempt to force the communists to break the deadlock over the POWs, Clark ordered increased air attacks over North Korea, and the bombings destroyed major hydroelectric plants on the Yalu River.

In the fall of 1952, Dwight D. Eisenhower was elected president of the United States, taking office in January 1953. Just a few months later, the Russian leader Joseph Stalin died, and the Soviet officials began to urge a peaceful settlement to the Korean situation. Finally, in April 1953, peace talks resumed, and the communists agreed to voluntary repatriation of POWs supervised by a commission made up of representatives from five neutral countries. A truce between the United Nations and North Korea was finally signed on July 27, 1953. South Koreans, however, opposed the armistice. They wanted to continue fighting in order to defeat the communists in North Korea.

Although the armistice brought a cease-fire, there was no real peace treaty. More than four decades later, in 1995, the war was technically not yet over because no permanent agreement had been signed. Over the years the arms buildup, banned by the armistice, continued unchecked.

Korea remains bitterly divided, and armies on both sides guard the DMZ, an area two and a half miles wide that crosses the peninsula.

In the late 1960s, while the United States was involved in the Vietnam War, guerrilla and terrorist attacks against South Koreans and American soldiers broke out along the DMZ. Although the ROK guarded most of southern boundary, U.S. armed forces patrolled an eighteen-mile section, which Major Vandon E. Jenerette called "a nearly forgotten place where soldiers . . . were engaged in combat operations on a smaller scale, but no less deadly, than the operations faced during the same period by fellow 'grunts' in Vietnam." He noted that as the United States became increasingly involved in the Vietnam War, "the tempo of incidents and violations of the Korean armistice also increased. Though it was not readily apparent at the time, there was speculation of a connection between the war in Southeast Asia and hostile acts committed by the North Koreans."

During the 1960s, sporadic confrontations between North Korean and U.S. soldiers forced Americans to focus occasionally on the yet-to-be-resolved Korean conflict. "American reaction at home to the provocations of the communists was rather mixed," Major Jenerette reported. "The media focus was on the war in Vietnam and reports of US combat operations and casualties in Korea, apparently, were not considered 'page one' subject matter."[5]

Since the 1970s, the war in Korea has been overshadowed by battles on other world fronts, prompting many American veterans of the Korean conflict to label it the Forgotten War. Some veterans believe the country has forgotten them, too, and has never properly recognized them. Yet, as one survivor of a North Korean ambush along the DMZ put it: "We did what the country asked us to do . . . that's all."[6]

*The inscription to the Korean War Memorial reads:*
*"Our nation honors her sons and daughters who answered the call*
*to defend a country they never knew and a people they never met. "*

Finally, on July 27, 1995, in Washington, D.C., U.S. veterans of the Korean War were honored with a memorial, which President Bill Clinton called "a magnificent reminder of what is best about the United States." In his remarks, President Clinton praised the dedication of the one and a half million Americans who helped to defend freedom:

> Tens of thousands of Americans died in Korea. Our South Korean allies lost hundreds of thousands of soldiers and civilians. Our other U.N. allies suffered grievous casualties. Thousands of Americans who were lost in Korea to this day have never been accounted for. . . .
>
> On this day 42 years ago, President Dwight Eisenhower called the end of hostilities an armistice on a single battleground, not peace in the world. It's fair to say that when the guns fell silent then, no one knew for sure what our forces in Korea had done for the future of our nation or the future of world freedom. The larger conflict of the Cold War had only begun. It would take four decades more to win.
>
> In a struggle so long and consuming, perhaps it's not surprising that too many lost sight of the importance of Korea. But now we know with the benefit of history, that those of you who served and the families who stood behind you laid the foundations for one of the greatest triumphs in the history of human freedom. By sending a clear message that America had not defeated fascism to see communism prevail, you put the free world on the road to victory in the Cold War. That is your enduring contribution. And all free people everywhere should recognize it today.[7]

# Source Notes

## One

1. Donald K. Chung, M.D., *The Three Day Promise* (Tallahassee, Fla.: Father and Son Publishing, Inc., 1989), 50.

2. Ibid. 94–95.

3. Ibid., 110.

4. Quoted in Henry Chang, ed., *Six Insides From the Korean War* (Seoul: Dae-Dong Moon Hwa Sa, 1958), 43.

5. Ibid., 44–45.

## Two

1. Quoted in Chang, *Six Insides*, 35.

2. Ibid., 57.

3. Keyes Beech, *Tokyo and Points East* (Garden City, N.Y.: Doubleday and Company, 1954), 114.

4. Quoted in John W. Riley Jr. and Wilbur Schramm, translations by Hugh Heung-wu Cynn, *The Reds Take a City* (New Brunswick, N.J.: Rutgers University Press, 1951), 48.

5. Ibid., 50.

6. Quoted in Chang, *Six Insides*, 66–67.

## Three

1. Quoted in Allen Guttman, ed., *Korea: Cold War and Limited War* (Lexington, Mass.: D.C. Heath and Company, 1972), 5.

2. Quoted in Geoffrey C. Ward, "Douglas MacArthur," *National Geographic*, March 1992, 80.

3. Quoted in Robert Leckie, *The War in Korea, 1950–1953* (Eau Claire, Wisc.: E. M. Hale and Company, 1963), 44.

4. Quoted in Rudy Tomedi, *No Bugles, No Drums: An Oral History of the Korean War* (New York: John Wiley & Sons, 1993), 5.

5. Quoted in Chung, *The Three Day Promise*, 112.

### Four

1. Chung, *The Three Day Promise*, 115–116.

2. Lt. Col. Charles M. Bussey, USA (Ret.), *Firefight at Yechon: Courage and Racism in the Korean War* (McClean, Va.: Brassey's, 1991), 99.

3. Ibid., 107.

4. Quoted in Don Lawson, *The United States in the Korean War* (New York: Scholastic Book Service, 1964), 39–40.

5. Quoted in Leckie, *The War in Korea*, 75–76.

6. Quoted in Lawson, *The United States in the Korean War*, 41.

### Five

1. Max Miller, *I'm Sure We've Met Before* (New York: E. P. Dutton & Company, Inc., 1951), 96.

2. Ibid., 97–98.

3. Harry G. Summers Jr., *Korean War Almanac* (New York: Facts On File, 1990), 142.

4. Miller, *I'm Sure We've Met Before*, 101.

5. Quoted in Joseph C. Goulden, *Korea: The Untold Story of the War* (New York: Times Books, 1982), 215.

6. General Paik Sun Yuk, *From Pusan to Panmunjom* (New York: Brassey's, 1992), 55–56.

### Six

1. Paik, *From Pusan*, 72–73.

2. Ibid., 84.

3. Quoted in Russell Spurr, *Enter the Dragon: China's Undeclared War Against the U.S. in Korea, 1950–1951* (New York: Newmarket Press, 1988), 261.

4. Beech, *Tokyo*, 185.

### Seven

1. James A. Frowein, e-mail correspondence with Martin Gay, May 28, 1995.

2. Quoted in Tomedi, *No Bugles*, 129.

3. Quoted in John Toland, *In Mortal Combat: Korea, 1950–1953* (New York: William Morrow, 1991), 258.

4. Ibid., 261.

5. Vandon E. Jenerette, "The Forgotten DMZ," Military Review, May 1988, 32–43, electronic posting on the "Korean War Project" at <http://www.onramp.net/~hbarker/index.html>

6. Ibid.

7. The White House Office of the Press Secretary, "Remarks by President Clinton and President Kim of South Korea," press release, July 27, 1995.

# For Further Information

## Books

Bachrach, Deborah. *The Korean War*. San Diego, Cal.: Lucent Books, 1991.

Brady, James P. *The Coldest War: A Memoir of Korea*. New York: Crown, 1990.

Donovan, Robert J. *Nemesis: Truman and Johnson in the Coils of War in Asia*. New York: St. Martin's Press, 1984.

Duncan, David. *This Is War: A Photo Narrative of the Korean War*. Boston: Little, Brown, 1990.

Dunstan, Simon. *Armour of the Korean War 1950–1953*. Harrisburg, Pa.: Stackpole, 1993.

Dvorchak, Robert J. *The Battle for Korea: The Associated Press History of the Korea Conflict*. Harrisburg, Pa.: Stackpole, 1993.

Fehrenbach, T. R. *The Fight for Korea: From the War of 1950 to the Pueblo Incident*. New York: Price, Stern, Sloan, 1969.

Higgins, Marguerite. *War in Korea*. New York: Doubleday, 1951.

Iserman, Maurice. *The Korean War*. New York: Facts On File, 1992.

Lyle, Rishell. *With a Black Platoon in Combat: A Year in Korea*. College Station, Tex.: Texas A&M University Press, 1993.

McGowen, Tom. *The Korean War.* New York: Franklin Watts, 1992.

Smith, Carter. *The Korean War.* Morristown, N.J.: Silver Burdett, 1990.

Soderbergh, Peter A. *Women Marines in the Korean War Era.* Westport, CT: Greenwood, 1994.

Stein, R. Conrad. *The Korean War: "The Forgotten War."* Springfield, N.J.: Enslow, 1994.

Tomedi, Rudy. *No Bugles, No Drums: An Oral History of the Korean War.* New York: Wiley, 1993.

### *A/V and CD-ROM*

*Korea, The Forgotten War* (92 min.) Los Angeles, Cal.: Fox Hills Video, 1987. Documentary using archival film footage. Grades 5–8.

*Mig Alley* (60 min.) Oak Park, Ill.: MPI Home video, © 1990. Aerial attacks of the Korean War, focusing on Mig Alley, a combat zone in Northwest Korea. Grades 5–8.

*That War in Korea* (ca. 75 min.) New York, N.Y.: Ambrose Video Pub., © 1990. Coverage of the Korean War, including background events. Grades 5–8.

# Index

Almond, Edward, 40
atom bomb, 20, 48
Australia, 22, 32

Beech, Keyes, 14–16, 45
Belgium, 22
black soldiers, 27–28, 49–50
Blair, Clay, 28
bombing of North Korea, 20, 26
Bussey, Charles M., 27–28

Canada, 22
China, 12, 19, 20, 40–46, 48–50
Chosin Reservoir, 44, 45
Chung, Donald, 6, 8–9, 26
Clark, Mark W., 54
Clinton, Bill, 57
cold war, 19, 57
Colombia, 22
communism, 9, 19
Craig, Edward, 29

Dean, William, 22, 23, 24
Denmark, 22
Dyer, Nell, 52

Eisenhower, Dwight D., 54, 57
Ethiopia, 22

France, 22
Frowein, James A., 48

Gay, Hobart, 37–38, 42
Great Britain, 5, 19, 32, 37, 41
Greece, 22

Heartbreak Ridge, 51
Higgins, Marguerite, 14, 16, 36–37, 45

Inchon landing, 33–39, 40
India, 22
Italy, 5, 22

Japan, 5–6, 13
Jenerette, Vandon E., 55
Joint Chiefs of Staff, 34, 40

Kean, William, 29
Kim Chonggi, 5, 10–11, 13–14, 17–18
Kim Il Sung, 8, 9, 13, 17, 42
Kim Yonggi, 5, 9–10, 13
Korea, partition of, 6–8

Lambert, Tom, 28
Lee, Kun-Ho, 16–17
Luxembourg, 22

MacArthur, Douglas, 20–23, 34– 37, 40, 42–44, 46–49
Marines, U.S., 28–30, 32–34, 36, 40–41, 44–45
Marshall, George, 40
Masan campaign, 28–29
Meatgrinder, 49
Miller, Max, 33–34, 36
Miryang, 29–30

No-Name Ridge, 29–30
North Korean People's Army (NKPA), 12, 16, 23, 24, 29–32, 37, 40, 43

Operation Chromite, 33
Osan, 23–24

Paik Sun Yup, 37–38, 41, 43
Partridge, Earl, 25
peace talks, 50–54
Philippines, 22, 41
prisoners of war (POWs), 23, 24, 51–54
Pusan Perimeter, 22–25, 28–32, 36, 37
Pyongyang, 8, 41

refugees, 14–16, 17–18, 24, 46
Rhee, Syngman, 7, 9, 12, 16, 25, 39
Ridgway, Matthew B., 48–49, 54
ROK troops, 8, 10, 12, 13, 16, 25, 32, 37–38, 40, 41, 43, 44, 55
Roy, Robert, 23

Seoul, 49
    fall and occupation of, 12–17
    recapture of, 36, 37, 39, 40
Sicily, 33–34, 36
Smith, Charles, 22, 23
Smith, Oliver, 44
Soviet Union, 5, 6, 7, 8, 12, 19, 20, 48, 54

Stalin, Joseph, 6, 17, 54
suicide attacks, 30–31
Summers, Harry, Jr., 35

Taegu, 25, 28–29, 30
Taejon, 22, 23, 24
Taiwan, 20
Task Force Smith, 22–24
Thailand, 22, 41
38th parallel, 6–7, 38
    crossed by UN troops, 40, 42, 46, 49, 50
    North Korean advance across, 10–13, 19
Truman, Harry S., 19, 20, 21–22, 42–43, 46–48
Turkey, 22, 41

United Kingdom, 22
United Nations (UN), 7, 19–20, 22, 39, 40, 54

Van Fleet, James A., 49, 50
veterans, 55–57
Vietnam War, 55

Walker, Walton H., 25, 27, 28–29, 32, 37, 48
White, Ted, 49–50
Wolmi-do, 33–34, 36
women, as correspondents, 14, 16, 36–37, 45
Wonsan, 40
World War II, 5–6, 12, 14, 29

X Corps, 37, 40–41, 43–44, 46, 49

Yalu River, 41, 43, 44, 54
Yechon Battle, 26–28
"yo-yo war," 48–50